Love: The Greatest Force in The Wonderment of The Human Experience

A Book of Tribute

And For Gifting to Someone You Love

Kevin Unruh

BookLocker

Trenton, Georgia

Print ISBN: 978-1-958878-41-5
Ebook ISBN: 979-8-88531-401-5

Published by BookLocker.com, Inc., Trenton, Georgia.

BookLocker.com, Inc.
2024

First Edition

Library of Congress Cataloging in Publication Data
Unruh, Kevin
Love: The Greatest Force in The Wonderment of The Human Experience
by Kevin Unruh
Library of Congress Control Number: 2022922473

Other Books by the Author

Ethics, Reason, & Excellence:
A Simple Formula for Leadership

Happiness Demystified:
How to Live a Happier Life

To my many kind and loving friends –
who make life so much more worthwhile

Contents

Introduction

Love is the most powerful force in the universe of human emotions. This book is intended as a reminder of this fact. A reminder of what it *can* do. What it *should* do. What it *does*. This book is a tribute to the power of love itself. It is also intended as a gift to be given to someone you love – to any family member, friend, partner, spouse, significant other, or any other person you love.

To the purchaser:

As you will see from the table of contents, the chapters in this book address many kinds of love and human relationships, with a special section at the end for writing down in your own words and in your own handwriting your feelings of love and gratitude for them. In each chapter are numerous quotations about love relevant to each chapter, and below each quotation is a blank line for your name or initials, which you can use to indicate to the person you bought this book for that this quotation is intended especially for them.

To the receiver:

You have received this book because you are loved in a very special way. This book is a tribute to you, specifically.

Date _____

This book of love is presented to _____

From _____

Love *is* the most powerful force in the human world.
Use it well. Use it often…

~

Chapter 1

The Gift of Love

There are many, many ways to describe love, of course, but the best way, I think, is to call it a gift. It is a gift of the human mind, of the mind-body-spirit, of the heart, and of the soul. The gift of love is a gift of *Self*, and there is no gift greater than this.

Being deeply loved by someone gives you strength,
while loving someone deeply gives you courage.[1]

— Lao Tzu

_____
your name/initials

The only thing we never get enough of is love;
and the only thing we never give enough of is love.[2]

— Henry Miller

_____
your name/initials

Chapter 2
Packaging

The gift of love, the gift of *Self* can be given in many forms and by many means. One's *time* is an excellent expression of love, as is one's devotion, loyalty, consideration, protection, support, patience, leadership, guidance, care, and assistance, among many others. However you choose to give it is not particularly important. All that is important is *that* you give it.

Keep love in your heart. A life without it is like a sunless garden when the flowers are dead.[3]

– Oscar Wilde

_____
your name/initials

Love is a better master than duty.[4]

– Albert Einstein

_____
your name/initials

Whenever you are confronted with an opponent, conquer him with love.[5]

– Mahatma Gandhi

_____
your name/initials

4

Chapter 3
The Purest Form

The purest expression of love – rather, the most principled and noble expression of love is *sacrifice:* to love someone more than you love yourself and to demonstrate it with a pure-hearted and one-sided exchange: an exchange of your own interests for theirs.

As humans, it is only natural to want and, sometimes, even to *expect* our love to be reciprocated. We are human, after all – and that's just how humans are made. But in the hierarchy of expressions of love, the purest form of love is undoubtedly sacrifice: giving what is *not* asked of you without self-interest and for no other reason than to do so for the benefit of the person you love. *This* is pure love. This is *true* love.

Love is that condition in which the happiness of another is essential to your own.[6]

– Robert A. Heinlein [Stranger In A Strange Land, *Chapter 4*]

---
your name/initials

Chapter 4

Another Level of Purity

We humans love children, and we love them purely. Many of us love our pets just as purely. That is, we love them – children and pets – with no ulterior motives. We do this because they are innocent and because we feel an innate need to protect them. We love them because it is right and good and nurturing and kind.

But we do not tend to do this as often – rarely, in fact – where adults are concerned. Where adults are concerned, we base our decisions to bestow love, acceptance, forbearance, and other such generosities that we afford children and pets on whether we perceive these adults to *deserve* our expressions of love. We often decide that we will not be kind or generous to someone that has not been kind to us or who is simply someone we perceive as unworthy of our love. But, like *sacrifice*, another higher order of love is love that we choose to give *in spite of* the worthiness we assign to the other person. It is love for the *sake* of love, for the sake of virtue – because we can.

Forgiveness is an example of this kind of love. Often people do not "deserve" our forgiveness, but we forgive them because we can and because to do so is magnanimous: love given for no other reason than because it is gracious and noble. Loving our peers the same as we love children and our animal companions is the pinnacle of purity in love.

Where all desires, emotion, time, energy, cause, effect,
and arguments fall, Pure Love evolves.[7]

– Bikramjit Konwar

your name/initials

6

Anyone can love a thing because. That's as easy as putting a penny in your pocket. But to love something despite. To know the flaws and love them too. That is rare and pure and perfect.[8]

– Patrick Rothfuss

_____
your name/initials

A drop of Pure Love contains an ocean of transformative power.[9]

– Adiela Akoo

_____
your name/initials

Chapter 5
Love as a Higher Principle

Ninety-nine percent of the time, love involves some form of direct interaction with another person or another living creature. But, sometimes, when applied in the most selfless way possible, love is given because of the inherent goodness found in the *principle* of love. Giving to charities, to the homeless, or to your fellow man are a few examples of love merely for the principle of it. The principle of love, in these instances, is as powerful as love gets because it is truly selfless, wanting nothing in return. I often think of this kind of love, this *motive* for expressing love as a tribute to love itself. Love is the greatest of all human emotions and to my mind deserves our reverence and admiration and – perhaps more than anything else – our dedication to its proliferation.

You will learn a lot about yourself if you stretch in the direction of goodness, of bigness, of kindness, of forgiveness, of emotional bravery. Be a warrior for love.[10]

– Cheryl Strayed

_____
your name/initials

Power at its best is love implementing the demands of justice, and justice at its best is power correcting everything that stands against love.[11]

– Martin Luther King, Jr. ["Where Do We Go From Here" sermon, 1967]

_____

your name/initials

9

Chapter 6
Gratitude

One of the most beautiful expressions of love there is comes in the form of gratitude. It *honors* the person you love by expressing your appreciation for them. If you truly love someone – in whatever form that love may take – then it is only natural, it is only logical that you would feel grateful for them.

We often tell people that we love them, and that is always a good thing. But, expressing gratitude for those we love is often appreciated even more because gratitude tends to identify the details of *why* we love someone. In the same sense that apologies are perceived as more sincere when we add to them the particulars of our regrets, gratitude also adds a more profound sense of sincerity to our more common expressions of love. "I love you," is one of the most beautiful expressions in all human language. Gratitude, though, infuses the love we express with *why*.

Appreciation is a wonderful thing. It makes what is excellent in others belong to us as well.[12]

– Voltaire

_____
your name/initials

Feeling gratitude and not expressing it is like wrapping a present and not giving it.[13]

– William Arthur Ward

_____
your name/initials

Chapter 7
Romantic Love

We tend to rank romantic love above all the other kinds. Perhaps because of the nature of passion, perhaps because it stirs the highest highs and the most heart-breaking lows, or perhaps because it often results in the union of two people in a way that no other form of love does. Whatever the case, it is a beautiful, rapturous, *upending* experience that poets, authors, everyday adults, and adolescents alike write about, talk about, and think about more than any other subject. If there is anything that causes more joy, more tumult, and more raw emotion than romantic love, I cannot name it. It is no wonder, really, that we place it on the highest pedestal. And to those that approach romantic love with an attitude of abandon, I tip my hat and place them on the highest pedestal, as well.

Of all forms of caution, caution in love is perhaps the most fatal to true happiness.[14]

– Bertrand Russell *[The Conquest of Happiness]*

———————————
your name/initials

If I had a flower for every time I thought of you... I could walk through my garden forever.[15]

– Alfred Tennyson

———————————
your name/initials

You are the finest, loveliest, tenderest, and most beautiful person I have ever known and even that is an understatement.[16]

– F. Scott Fitzgerald

_{your name/initials}

If I know what love is, it is because of you.[17]

– Hermann Hesse

_{your name/initials}

My soul and your soul are forever tangled.[18]

– N.R. Hart

_{your name/initials}

Because of you, I can feel myself slowly, but surely, becoming the me I have always dreamed of being.[19]

– Tyler Knott Gregson

_{your name/initials}

Your hand touching mine. This is how galaxies collide.[20]

— Sanober Khan

_____
your name/initials

I swear I couldn't love you more than I do right now, and yet I know I will tomorrow.[21]

— Leo Christopher

_____
your name/initials

You know you're in love when you can't fall asleep because reality is finally better than your dreams.[22]

— Dr. Seuss

_____
your name/initials

Chapter 8
Friendship Love

Romantic love gets the most press, naturally, but the love of one friend for another, while a love-bond of a different form, is no less profound. And though all forms of love are beautiful, of course, it can be argued – *and has been* – that friendship love is perhaps the purest form of all.

Rare as is true love, true friendship is rarer.[23]

– Jean de La Fontaine

_____
your name/initials

To love well is the task in all meaningful relationships, not just in romantic bonds.[24]

– bell hooks [All About Love: New Visions]

_____
your name/initials

Let us be grateful to people who make us happy; they are the charming gardeners who make our souls blossom.[25]

– Marcel Proust

_____
your name/initials

One loyal friend is worth ten thousand relatives.[26]

– Euripides

_____
your name/initials

Each friend represents a world in us, a world not born until they arrive, and it is only by this meeting that a new world is born.[27]

– Anais Nin

_____
your name/initials

Friendship is unnecessary, like philosophy, like art... It has no survival value; rather it is one of those things that gives value to survival.[28]

– C. S. Lewis

_____
your name/initials

The sincere friends of this world are as ship lights in the stormiest of nights.[29]

– Giotto di Bondone

_____
your name/initials

Nothing but heaven itself is better than a friend who is really a friend.[30]

– Plautus

_____
your name/initials

Friends... they cherish one another's hopes. They are kind to one another's dreams.[31]

– Henry David Thoreau

_____
your name/initials

There is nothing on this earth more to be prized than true friendship.[32]

– Thomas Aquinas

_____
your name/initials

Chapter 9
Family

The love of family is like no other. It is innate, profound, and indelible. Parents are our first role models, champions, and protectors; brothers and sisters are our first friends, confidants, and team members; and grandparents are very often our first sense of history, of family identity, and of family pride. Love of family gives us a sense of belonging, a sense of security, and a comforting sense of foundation that we do not get as deeply from any other source. The love of family is the beginning of our understanding of love, supports us through the evolution of our lives, and sustains us until the end. The love of family is like no other.

Mothers

Mama was my greatest teacher, a teacher of compassion, love, and fearlessness. If love is sweet as a flower, then my mother is that sweet flower of love.[33]

– Stevie Wonder

_____
your name/initials

An ounce of mother is worth a pound of clergy.[34]

– Rudyard Kipling

_____
your name/initials

17

I can imagine no heroism greater than motherhood.[35]

– Lance Conrad

_____
your name/initials

A mother understands what a child does not say.[36]

– A Jewish proverb

_____
your name/initials

Fathers

My father didn't tell me how to live;
he lived and let me watch him do it.[37]

– Clarence Budington Kelland

_____
your name/initials

One father is more than a hundred schoolmasters.[38]

– George Herbert

_____
your name/initials

Everything my mother and father did
was designed to put me where I am.[39]

– Henry Louis Gates

_____
your name/initials

I am not ashamed to say that no man I ever met was my father's equal,
and I never loved any other man as much.[40]

– Hedy Lamarr

_____
your name/initials

Sisters

I do not see as well without her. I do not hear as well without her. I do
not feel as well without her. I would be better off without a hand or a
leg than without my sister.[41]

– Erin Morgenstern

_____
your name/initials

For there is no friend like a sister in calm or stormy weather; To cheer one on the tedious way, To fetch one if one goes astray, To lift one if one totters down, To strengthen whilst one stands.[42]

– Christina Rossetti

_____
your name/initials

Sweet is the voice of a sister in the season of sorrow.[43]

– Benjamin Disraeli

_____
your name/initials

There can be no situation in life in which the conversation of my dear sister will not administer some comfort to me.[44]

– Mary Worley Montagu

_____
your name/initials

Brothers

There is no love like the love for a brother. There is no love like the love from a brother.[45]

– Astrid Alauda

_____
your name/initials

It takes two men to make one brother.[46]

– Israel Zangwill

---
your name/initials

Stop for a moment and realize how lucky you are to have one.[47]

– Max Lagacé

---
your name/initials

He ain't heavy, he's my brother.[48]

– James Wells

---
your name/initials

Grandparents

Grandparents can be very special resources. Just being close to them reassures a child, without words, about change and continuity, about what went before and what will come after.[49]

– Fred Rogers

---
your name/initials

If God had intended us to follow recipes, He wouldn't have given us grandmothers.[50]

– Linda Henley

<small>your name/initials</small>

No spring, nor summer hath such grace, as I have seen in one autumnal face.[51]

– John Donne

<small>your name/initials</small>

Sons/Daughters

Sons are the anchors of a mother's life.[52]

– Sophocles

<small>your name/initials</small>

A man ain't nothing but a man. But a son? Well, now, that's somebody.[53]

— Toni Morrison

_____
your name/initials

You are my angel. You remind me of the goodness in this world and inspire me to be the greatest version of myself.[54]

— Steve Maraboli

_____
your name/initials

Life is tough, my darling, but so are you.[55]

— Stephanie Bennet Henry

_____
your name/initials

Nieces/Nephews/Cousins

Nieces and nephews are exactly like the children I would've chosen to be my kids, if I had chosen to be a parent, which I didn't – because I already had such great nieces and nephews.

— Me

_____
your name/initials

Kevin Unruh

I really enjoy being an uncle. I basically get to rent out the kids for free, have almost no responsibility, get to be funny and act cool, and get to buy them frivolous things for which I get 10X more credit than their parents get for all the boring stuff they have to buy them – you know, for education and survival and stuff.

– Me

_____
your name/initials

Nieces and nephews are familial gifts that afford us the wonderful opportunity of loving two people at once: the child themselves and the brother or sister that made us the aunt or uncle.

– Me

_____
your name/initials

A good cousin is like having a bonus brother or sister. Who doesn't love a good cousin?

– Me

_____
your name/initials

There often exists a family member that isn't technically a brother or sister but who, due to the many convolutions and vagaries of some family dynamics, is even better than a brother or sister. And that person is often a cousin.

– Me

_____
your name/initials

Chosen Family

Blood does not family make. Those are relatives. Family are those with whom you share your good, bad, and ugly and still love one another in the end. Those are the ones you select.[56]

– Hector Xtravaganza

_____
your name/initials

Chapter 10
Love Can

Love is the most powerful of all human emotions because it can do so many wonderful things…

It can move people to tears of joy.
It can move them to tears of sorrow.
It can heal pain.
It can lift the downhearted.
It can soften one's heart and the hearts of others.
It can give hope.
It can engender fairness, objectivity, and kindness.
It can produce forbearance, understanding, and patience.
It can forgive and mend.
It can enlighten, rescue, and transform.
It is the only emotion that can defeat hate.
It can change people and moments and life.

Love is the greatest force in the wonderment of the human experience. May you receive it in abundance. May you give it even more generously…

~

A Letter of Love/Gratitude

Dear _____,

I bought this book for you because I love you/am grateful for you and wanted to tell you so in writing...

_____

_____

_____

_____

_____

_____

_____

_____

_____

_____

_____

_____

_____

_____

_____

_____

_____

_____

_____

_____

Husband/Wife/Partner/Boyfriend/Girlfriend/ Significant Other Section

_____, I still love you just as much as I did before you lost all the money we set aside for a vacation house in the stupid crypto market.

_____
your name/initials

_____, most women smell pretty good, but you smell like love mixed with frosting.

_____
your name/initials

Before I met you, I told myself I would always have a separate bathroom when I got married. Now... well, that was before I met you. Now, a separate bathroom just sounds lonely.

_____
your name/initials

_____, I love you even though you have never learned how to load the dishwasher, fold clothes, or shut drawers and cabinet doors.

_____
your name/initials

_____, I love you even though there is always a fresh tangle of hair stuck to the shower wall each and every day.

_____
your name/initials

_____, I love you even though you continue to try to fool me into eating kale.

_____
your name/initials

I love you, _____, even though you sometimes dance in public.

_____
your name/initials

_____, I love you because you are always willing to turn up the heat when we are watching Netflix, even though you are already sweating under the blanket.

_____
your name/initials

_____, I love you because my cat loves you.

_____
your name/initials

_____, I love you because my dog loves you.

_____
your name/initials

_____, I love you because you make me feel good about me.

_____
your name/initials

_____, I love you because you treat my family like gold.

_____
your name/initials

_____, I love you because you are always you.

_____
your name/initials

I love you, _____, and I don't even care if you say it back.

_____
your name/initials

I love you, _____, and you *better* say it back.

_____
your name/initials

_____, I love you. That's all. I just love you.

_____
your name/initials

Grandparents Section

_____, I would love you just as much even if you didn't make the best _____ [← insert kind] pie in the entire world.

_____
your name/initials

_____, I would love you just as much even if you didn't give me the money my parents asked you to stop giving me.

_____
your name/initials

_____, I love you even though you still don't know how to text and the only emoji you know is the one you hit by accident three years ago.

_____
your name/initials

_____, I would love you just as much even if you didn't think I was the most beautiful child you have ever seen.

_____
your name/initials

_____, I would love you just as much even if you didn't come rescue me every time I run out of gas.

_____
your name/initials

_____, I love you because even though you don't care for the way I wear my hair or the way I dress, you still know that I am a good kid.

_____
your name/initials

_____, I love you. That's all. I just love you.

_____
your name/initials

Grandma/Grandpa,

_____

_____

_____

_____

_____

_____

_____

_____

_____

_____

_____

_____

_____

<u>Mom/Dad Section</u>

_____, I love you even though you have no ability to remain silent about the boys I date.

_____
your name/initials

_____ I love you even though you call me 11 times a day.

_____
your name/initials

_____, I love you even though you told me that I "couldn't pull off" that dress I was so in love with.

_____
your name/initials

_____, I love you even though I am _____ [insert age] and you still tell me what time I should go to bed.

_____
your name/initials

_____, I love you even though you make fun of me because I don't know how to work on cars.

_____
your name/initials

_____, I love you. That's all. I just love you.

_____
your name/initials

Mom/Dad,

_____

_____

_____

_____

_____

_____

_____

_____

_____

_____

_____

_____

_____

_____

_____

_____

_____

_____

_____

_____

_____

<u>Brother/Sister Section</u>

_____, I still love you even though you used to beat me up and sometimes still seem to want to.

_____
your name/initials

Brother with 50+ tattoos, I still love you even though you still try to run off every guy I date that has more than *one* tattoo.

_____
your name/initials

Brother, I still love you even though I have at least five girlfriends that won't speak to me anymore because of you.

_____
your name/initials

_____, I love you even though you never got in trouble for *the very same things* Mom and Dad yelled at *me* about.

_____
your name/initials

Sister, you have at least 23 items of clothing that we both know you stole from me. But I love you anyway because I know it could have been 50.

_____
your name/initials

_____, I love you even though you're smarter and prettier and better than me but treat me like *I* am the golden child.

_____
your name/initials

_____, I love you even though you told Mom I smoke weed.

_____
your name/initials

_____, I love you. That's all. I just love you.

_____
your name/initials

Brother/Sister,

_____

_____

_____

_____

_____

_____

_____

_____

_____

_____

Son/Daughter Section

Well, _____, The truth is you are not what I was hoping for. Luckily, you took after your mother, and you came out *much better* than expected. You're a good human, and I love you.

_____
your name/initials

Most every parent loves their children, but you, _____, *you* are loved, appreciated, and truly cherished. You make being a Mom/Dad the greatest job on Earth.

_____
your name/initials

I am not going to lie to you, _____: You were absolutely, 100% an "accident" – and the best thing that ever happened to me/us. I love you.

_____
your name/initials

I can't say that I've done a whole lot of things right in my life, but you, _____ ...well, I have to say *you* I got right. You're one great kid. I love you.

_____
your name/initials

_____, I love you. That's all. I just love you.

_____
your name/initials

Aunt/Uncle Section

Thank you for all you do for me/us. You are one of the most important people in my/our life, and this family would not be the same without you.

_____
your name/initials

_____, I love you. That's all. I just love you.

_____
your name/initials

<u>Other Significant Family Member</u>

_____, I love you. We may not have common blood, but you're as much a part of me/us as the rest of the family.

_____
your name/initials

_____, I love you. That's all. I just love you.

_____
your name/initials

Acknowledgements

For your keen eyes, excellent recommendations, thoroughness, care, and unflagging support, thank you KGP, Cheryl, Karla, Sneha, and Janice Lynne. You are always patient, kind, and wonderfully helpful.

Wait... *"Acknowledgements"*? In a book about love? Please disregard the title of this section (KGP, Cheryl, Karla, Sneha, and Janice Lynne). That's just for the public. For you, this section title should be "Love," but, as you can see, I am a very professional author, so for purposes of this book (and my precious professional credibility), I must hold fast with convention in displaying the present "Acknowledgements" header. But, please know that for all your efforts and generosity, not only are you *acknowledged*, but you are also supremely appreciated – *and loved.*

Notes

1. Harish. (2017, February 14). The Amazing Power of Love: Quotes and Musings. Launch Your Genius. https://www.launchyourgenius.com.
2. Ibid.
3. Ibid.
4. Ibid.
5. Ibid.
6. Jenkins, Cameron and Stansbury, Larry. (2022, August 19). 122 Best Love Quotes That Prove True Romance Really Does Exist. Original Source: Heinlein, Robert. *Stranger In A Strange Land.* [1961]. https://www.goodhousekeeping.com.
7. Goodreads. (n.d.) Pure Love Quotes. https://www.goodreads.com.
8. Roychoudhury, Rajnandini (2023, December 12). 100 Best Pure Love Quotes To Share With Someone Special. Edited by Monisha Kochhar. Kidadl. https://www.kidadl.com.
9. Ibid.
10. Vagianos, Alanna (2017, February 14). 21 Quotes That Show The Radical Power Of Love. Original Source: Strayed, Cheryl *Tiny Beautiful Things: Advice On Love And Life From Dear Sugar* [2012]. HuffPost. https://www.huffpost.com.
11. Ibid.
12. Lemire, Sarah and Zito, Barbara Bellisi (2022, July 28) 68 Gratitude Quotes To Express Your Deep Appreciation This Year. Today. https://www.today.com.
13. Ibid.
14. Niles, Mary (2024, February 5). 100+ Romantic Love Quotes for Her & Him To Say I Love You. Parade. https://www.parade.com.
15. Ibid.
16. Ibid.
17. Ibid.
18. Ibid.
19. Ibid.
20. Ibid.

21. Ibid.
22. Ibid.
23. BrainyQuote. (n.d.). Friendship Quotes. https://www.brainyquote.com.
24. Jenkins, Cameron and Stansbury, Larry. (2022, August 19). 122 Best Love Quotes That Prove True Romance Really Does Exist. Original Source: hooks, bell. *All About Love: New Visions.* [2018]. Good Housekeeping. https://www.goodhousekeeping.com.
25. BrainyQuote. (n.d.). Friendship Quotes. https://www.brainyquote.com.
26. Ibid.
27. Ibid.
28. Ibid.
29. Ibid.
30. Ibid.
31. Ibid.
32. Proflowers. (2020, August 19). 120 Friendship Quotes Your Best Friend Will Love. https://www.proflowers.com/blog/frienship-quotes.
33. BrainyQuote. (n.d.). Mother Quotes. https://www.brainyquote.com.
34. Ibid.
35. Goodreads. (n.d.) Lance Conrad Quotes. https://www.goodreads.com.
36. O'Dair, Barbara (2024, May 13). 100 Motherhood Quotes That Will Make You Want to Call Your Mom. Reader's Digest. https://www.rd.com/list/quotes-about-mothers/.
37. BrainyQuote. (n.d.). Father Quotes. https://www.brainyquote.com.
38. Ibid.
39. Ibid.
40. Ibid.
41. Parade (2024, March 29). 50 Sister Quotes That Will Make You Want to Call Her Right Now. Parade. https://www.parade.com.
42. Ibid.
43. Ibid.
44. Ibid.

45. Tingley, Lauren (2020, November 20). 36 Brother Quotes And Captions About Brotherly Love. Simply Well Balanced. https://www.simply-well-balanced.com.
46. Ibid.
47. Wisdom Quotes. (n.d.) 155 Brother Quotes That Will Make You Feel Lucky. https://www.wisdomquotes.com.
48. Ware, Michelle (2024, April 23). The Meaning Behind The Song "He Ain't Heavy, He's My Brother By The Hollies. [Based on a poem by the same name by James Wells.] Old Time Music. https://www.oldtimemusic.com
49. Sager, Jessica (2024, May 7). 150 Grandparents Quotes to Warm Your Heart and Remind You of Who Loves You the Most. Parade. https://www.parade.com/1259543/jessicasager/grandparents-quotes/.
50. Ibid.
51. Ibid.
52. Danao, Karen (n.d.) 80 Son Quotes to Reinforce Your Unending Love & Strong Bond. Quote Ambition. https://www.quoteambition.com.
53. Ibid.
54. Seale, Natalie (2024, March 14). Daughter Quotes. KeepInspiring.Me. https://www.keepinspiring.me.
55. Ibid.
56. Inspiring Quotes (n.d.) 13 Quotes About the Families We Choose. https://www.inspiringquotes.com.

Printed in the USA
CPSIA information can be obtained
at www.ICGtesting.com
JSHW080006220824
68270JS00005B/172